DATE DUE		

FEMALE FIRSTS IN THEIR FIELDS

Air & Space

Broadcasting & Journalism

Business & Industry

Entertainment & Performing Arts

Government & Politics

Literature

Science & Medicine

Sports & Athletics

FEMALE FIRSTS IN THEIR FIELDS

SCIENCE
&
MEDICINE

Gina De Angelis

Introduction by
Roslyn Rosen

CHELSEA HOUSE PUBLISHERS
Philadelphia

To Audrey:
May your story one day be even greater
than those in this book.

Produced by P. M. Gordon Associates, Inc.
Philadelphia, Pennsylvania

Editor in Chief Stephen Reginald
Managing Editor James D. Gallagher
Production Manager Pamela Loos
Art Director Sara Davis
Director of Photography Judy L. Hasday
Senior Production Editor Lisa Chippendale
Publishing Coordinator James McAvoy

Picture research by Artemis Picture Research Group, Inc.
Cover illustration by Cliff Spohn
Cover design by Keith Trego

Frontispiece: Marie Curie

The Chelsea House World Wide Web site address is
http://www.chelseahouse.com

3 5 7 9 8 6 4 2

Library of Congress Cataloging-in-Publication Data

DeAngelis, Gina.
    Female Firsts in their fields. Science and medicine / Gina DeAngelis.
       p. cm.
    Includes bibliographical references and index.
    Summary: Chronicles the lives and accomplishments of notable
women working in the fields of medicine and science in general,
including Marie Curie, Rachel Carson, and Margaret Mead.
    ISBN 0-7910-5143-9 (hardcover)
    1. Women scientists—Biography—Juvenile literature. 2. Women
medical scientists—Biography—Juvenile literature. [1. Scientists.
2. Women—Biography.] I. Title. II. Title: Science & Medicine.
III. Title: Science and medicine.
Q141.D32   1998
509.2'2—dc21
    [B]   98-31676
                                                              CIP
                                                               AC

CONTENTS

INTRODUCTION

Roslyn Rosen

When I was a toddler, it struck me that the other people in my family's New York apartment building were different. They did not use their hands when they talked, and they did not have to watch each other speak. I had been born deaf, and I felt sorry for them because they did not know the joy of drawing pictures in the air. They could not splash ideas into the air with a jab of the finger or a wave of the hand. Not until later did I realize the downside of being deaf–I couldn't communicate directly with my grandparents and extended family members, I depended on others to make important phone calls for me, and I found life's opportunities narrower, in part because I had few deaf (let alone female) role models.

Gallaudet University in Washington, D.C., is the only college for deaf students in the world. I arrived there in September 1958. It was a haven where sign language was part of the educational process, where there were deaf professors, and where opportunities for extracurricular leadership abounded. At Gallaudet I met deaf female professionals for the first time, although there were probably not more than three or four. The president and administrators of Gallaudet were all males who could hear–typical of school administrations during those years.

In my first month at Gallaudet, I also met the man who would become my husband. My destiny was charted: major in something that I could use as a homemaker (since that would be my job), get married, have a bunch of kids, and live happily ever after. This was the expectation for women in the late 1950s and early 1960s. And I stuck to the script: I majored in art with an emphasis on education and English, got married, and had three children. My life was complete—or so I thought.

The 1960s were turbulent and thought-provoking years. The civil rights movement and the beginnings of a women's movement emphasized human rights and equality for all. I came to see how alike the issues were that faced women, people of color, and people with disabilities, in terms of human rights and respect for human differences. Multicultural studies are vital for this understanding. Changes were occurring at an accelerating rate. Those changes affected my husband and me by broadening our traditional gender roles. With my husband's support, I pursued a master's degree in education of deaf students and later a doctoral degree in education administration. From my first job as a part-time sign language teacher, I eventually joined the faculty at Gallaudet University. In 1981 I was promoted to dean of the College for Continuing Education, and in 1993, to vice president for academic affairs.

During the formative years of my career, many of my role models and mentors were deaf men who had reached positions of leadership. They hired, taught, advised, and encouraged me. There were times when I felt the effects of the "glass ceiling" (an invisible barrier that keeps women or minorities from rising any higher). Sometimes I needed to depend on my male colleagues because my access to "old boy" networks or decision makers was limited. When I became involved with the National Association of the Deaf (NAD), the world's oldest organization of deaf people, I met deaf women who became role models—Dr. Gertie Galloway was the first deaf female president of the NAD, and Marcella Meyer had founded the Greater Los Angeles Community Service of the Deaf (GLAD). In 1980 I was elected to the board of directors of the National Association of the Deaf, and in 1990, I became the second woman elected president of NAD.

When I became a dean at Gallaudet in 1981, I also became a member of the school's Council of Deans, which at the time included only two deaf deans and two female deans. I was the only deaf woman dean. The vice president was a white male, and he once commented that top administrators often build management teams in their own image. I have found that to be true. As a dean, I was the highest-ranking deaf woman at Gallaudet, and I was able to hire and help a number of young deaf female professionals within the College for Continuing Education and our regional centers around the country. In the five years that I have been vice president at Gallaudet I have added many deaf, female, and minority members to my own management team. When I was the president of NAD, I hired its first deaf female executive director, Nancy Bloch. I also encouraged two of my friends, Mabs Holcomb and Sharon Wood, to write the first deaf women history book, a source of inspiration for young deaf girls.

It is important for women who have reached the top levels of their fields to advise and help younger women to become successful. It is also important for young girls to know about the groundbreaking contributions of women who came before them. The women profiled in this series of biographies overcame many obstacles to succeed. Some had physical handicaps, others fought generations of discriminatory attitudes toward women in the workplace. The world may never provide equal opportunities for every human being, but we can all work together to improve life for the next generation.

DR. ROSLYN ROSEN is the Vice President for Academic Affairs at Gallaudet University in Washington, D.C. Dr. Rosen has served as a board member and President of the National Association of the Deaf (NAD), the oldest consumer organization in the world, and was a member of the National Captioning Institute's executive board for nine years. She is currently a board member of the World Federation of the Deaf. Dr. Rosen also wears the hats of daughter, wife, mother, and proud grandmother.

ELIZABETH BLACKWELL

"Doctor Opens Office," said the advertisement in a New York newspaper. Nothing unusual about that. The ad went on to say that a Dr. Blackwell had graduated from Geneva Medical School in New York and was opening an office at University Place. Nothing unusual about that either. But the doctor to whom the ad referred was very unusual–Dr. *Elizabeth* Blackwell.

It was a time when women were expected to stay in the home and rear children, cook, and sew–and little else. There were, of course, women who taught school or performed other jobs that were considered "suitable," but the study of the human body? Of male as well as female organs? Such an idea was preposterous to most people. Women were too delicate for such work–they would surely faint, or worse, fail, and endanger the lives of their patients. Wouldn't they?

Elizabeth Blackwell was born in February 1821 near Bristol, England. She was the third child of five girls and four boys (although her mother had several more children who

Told her ambition to be a doctor was preposterous, Elizabeth Blackwell nevertheless graduated from medical school and opened her own practice.

did not survive). Samuel Blackwell, her father, was a sugar refiner who disliked the fact that his business depended on slave labor in the British West Indies. Hannah Lane Blackwell, her mother, was very religious; the couple were among those who dissented from the Church of England. (They were known as Dissenters and often held very liberal beliefs for that time.) Samuel believed in educating his girls in the same subjects as he did his boys, and not limiting them to the more conventional "girls" subjects like music and embroidery. This upbringing would have a profound effect on his children.

Samuel Blackwell moved to the United States with his family in August 1832. The family settled in Jersey City for a few years, and Elizabeth and the other children attended school in New York City.

In 1838 Samuel moved his family to Cincinnati, but he died a few months later, leaving his family close to destitution. The oldest girls, including Elizabeth, opened a day school under their mother's direction, to take in money. The eldest son, meanwhile, found himself a job outside the home.

Elizabeth taught in her family's school for several years, then took a teaching position in the tiny town of Henderson, Kentucky. She disliked the reality of slavery there, according to her autobiography, and left the town after only one term. On a trip home to Cincinnati, Elizabeth met an old family friend, Mary Donaldson, who apparently gave her the idea to be a doctor. Elizabeth was 24 and bored with teaching when the dying Mrs. Donaldson remarked to her, "If I could have been treated by a lady doctor, my worst suffering would have been spared me."

Almost immediately, in 1845, Elizabeth wrote to doctors and anyone else who might be willing and able to advise or help her. Most people, including Harriet Beecher Stowe, told her that her idea, at least for the time being, was preposterous and impossible. Those who did express sympathy with her idea were unable or unwilling to help, but this only made her more determined.

In the latter part of 1845 Elizabeth moved to Asheville, North Carolina, to be a music teacher; the family she was to board with was headed by a doctor, John Dickson, who agreed to teach her medicine. She spent the following years studying medicine with sympathetic doctors in Charleston and Philadelphia—then the capital of American medicine—and writing to colleges seeking admission as a medical student. She refused the advice of some people to disguise herself as a man so that she could attend Paris medical schools, because she wanted to open the profession to women. Dressing as a man would not serve such a purpose. Finally in 1847 she was accepted to Geneva Medical College in New York State. The students had been polled and had voted to allow her to study—perhaps expecting her to fail. Whatever the reason, Elizabeth found her classmates generally polite and even supportive of her efforts.

She made it through year one and returned to Philadelphia over the summer to work at Blockley Almshouse, a hospital for the poor. Here Elizabeth worked with women with syphilis and became adamant about two things: first, sanitation and hygiene, and second, educating women about their own bodies, health, and sex. This was a truly shocking attitude in her day. If feminine virtue and delicacy were to be protected, certainly women should not learn about the sexual organs, said the prevailing attitude of the day. But venereal diseases like syphilis are contracted by having sexual intercourse with infected persons, and Elizabeth was shocked that most women in the Almshouse had no idea how they had contracted such dangerous diseases. Education, she believed, was the key to prevention. "Feminine delicacy" was no excuse for ignorance that jeopardized women's health and lives.

Elizabeth Blackwell returned to Geneva for her second year of study and graduated in January 1849. Medical schools at the time required only a two-year course, consisting primarily of lectures and observation. Students were expected to work in a hospital to gain clinical experience after medical school. After graduation, Elizabeth had to find a hospital that would allow her to work. Also, she required several more years of study and training to fulfill her dream of becoming a surgeon.

Elizabeth went to Paris, where some of the best medical schools and hospitals in the world were located. But she had trouble finding a hospital that would allow her to practice her profession. Finally she was admitted to La Maternité, a hospital that trained midwives. She was only allowed to study as a midwife-trainee, like all the other women in the program, despite her medical degree. While studying there, Elizabeth met Hippolyte Blot, a young doctor with whom she may have been in love. Elizabeth knew, however, that her chosen career and the pressures of being the first woman to practice medicine would probably keep her from ever marrying.

While syringing a baby's eye at La Maternité, Elizabeth accidentally got a drop of the fluid in her own eye. She suffered intensely from the infection, which spread to both eyes and was so virulent that she had her left eye removed to save the vision in her right. This horrific experience ended her dreams of being a surgeon.

When she recovered, Elizabeth went to England to work and study at St. Bartholomew's Hospital in

London. She made a great number of friends, among them Florence Nightingale, not yet the famous nurse she would become.

Elizabeth wanted to stay in England but felt a duty to return to America and her family. She sailed to New York in 1851, where she soon encountered the attitudes she had found in Paris: there were no hospitals willing to have a female doctor on staff. At the time, the term "doctor" when applied to a woman meant "abortionist," and few landlords would let Dr. Blackwell rent their rooms or houses to set up practice. When she did acquire a small space, no patients came. Finally she decided to deliver lectures on the health and development of young women, which brought her enough attention to have some paying patients. These were mostly Quakers, who were very encouraging and supportive of Dr. Blackwell's efforts to help poor women who could not pay. She opened a dispensary in 1853 that became, about a year later, the New York Dispensary for Women and Children.

With Elizabeth's support, her younger sister was accepted to a medical school in Ohio and promised to come back and work with Elizabeth after she received her degree. Elizabeth also bought a house during this time and used it to set up practice.

In 1854, tired of her lonely personal life, Elizabeth adopted a young Irish orphan named Katherine Barry, called "Kitty." The girl remained a devoted companion of her adoptive mother until the end of her life. Around the same time, a young woman doctor named Marie Zakrzewska came to Elizabeth. She was new in the United States, and wanted Elizabeth's help.

Elizabeth's dispensary was already growing out of the house she had bought, and with the support of her influential Quaker friends she wanted to found

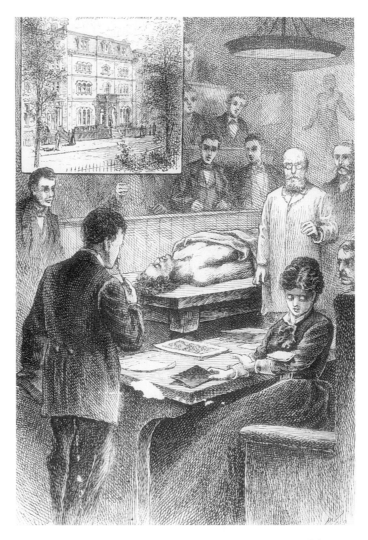

In her New York infirmary for women and children, Blackwell helped quiet public apprehension about female doctors by arranging for men to assist.

a hospital for women and children that would provide training specifically for female physicians. Her sister Emily Blackwell, who by now had received her degree and was in England studying medicine in a prestigious hospital, sent back large amounts of money she managed to raise there.

The New York Infirmary for Women and Children opened in a house on Bleecker Street that had been donated by Harriet Roosevelt. Emily Blackwell and Marie Zakrzewska came to New York to join the new hospital's staff.

The Infirmary was the first institution in the United States in which only women performed clinical duties. Nevertheless, the trustees of the institution were almost required to be men, in accordance with the overwhelming belief at the time that women were incapable of practicing medicine safely.

Although the women were excellent physicians, their success rate was not always perfect. But because they were women, when a patient died the male relatives and neighbors would often show up with weapons and accuse the women of murder. For this reason, Elizabeth had arranged for male physicians to assist the women in providing second opinions and reassuring the public that the female physicians were not quacks.

Emily and Marie ran the hospital very well, and this situation, combined with offers begging Elizabeth to come to England to work, made Elizabeth more willing to return to her beloved England. Elizabeth and Kitty arrived in summer 1858.

On January 1, 1859, Elizabeth Blackwell's name was entered on the United Kingdom's Medical Register; she was the first female to be listed there.

In 1860 Marie Zakrzewska, after two years' unpaid service, left the New York hospital to work at a hospital in Boston. Dr. Zakrzewska went on to found the New England Hospital for Women and Children. Elizabeth, by this time, was interested in founding a medical college for women. Her hospital continued to be a place where female doctors could gain experience after getting their degrees, however. For example, Rebecca Cole, the first black woman doctor, worked at the New York Infirmary.

When the Civil War began, Elizabeth helped train and interview nurses for the war, sending them on

In old age, Blackwell wrote her autobiography and continued to lecture on medical topics.

to Washington, D.C., where Dorothea Dix interviewed them and assigned them to battlefield hospitals. She continued to travel into New York City to help at the hospital.

Finally, the war ended, and Elizabeth founded a medical school for women. The school established an unprecedented four-year course—such a length of study was unheard-of even for male doctors. The course also centered on practical experience, not just on lectures and observations. The school opened in November 1868 and gave strict entrance exams to ensure quality students. It remained open until 1898, when it was decided that there was no longer any need for a medical school exclusively for women. During the intervening years, more than 4,000 women graduated from the school. (Unfortunately, the school's closing was followed by a drastic decline in the number of female graduates in medicine. The male-dominated medical profession apparently still viewed female doctors as business competition.)

In 1869 an exhausted Elizabeth finally moved to England permanently, bringing Kitty along. There she founded the London School of Medicine for Women and served as chair of gynecology, while continuing to write and deliver lectures. In 1895 Elizabeth wrote her autobiography, *Pioneer Work in Opening the Medical Profession to Women: Autobiographical Sketches*.

She and Kitty were vacationing in Kilmun, Scotland, in 1907 when Elizabeth fell down a flight of stairs. Although nothing was broken, Elizabeth never seemed to recover entirely from the accident (she was 86 at the time). She died at Kilmun on May 31, 1910, at age 88, after revolutionizing the Western medical profession and inspiring countless other women.

CLARA BARTON

One day in the 1850s, when a strong-willed female schoolteacher was offered a job, she testily replied, "I may sometimes be willing to teach for nothing, but if paid at all, I shall never do a man's work for less than a man's pay." The job was with the Oxford, Massachusetts school board, which was desperate for a teacher for the difficult winter term. Women schoolteachers were routinely paid less than men, but such was the young lady's talent that the school board relented and paid her the higher salary for the position.

This little woman, later earning the nickname "Angel of the Battlefield," had not always been so assertive. Born on Christmas Day, 1821, the youngest of six children, Clarissa Harlowe Barton was doted on but often exhibited a painful shyness and paralyzing timidity.

Her older brothers and sisters, and her parents, never failed to encourage her keen mind and strong curiosity. Even though most Americans at the time believed that girls should be taught easier subjects than boys, Clara's parents disagreed. Their determination to see that their daughters were edu-

Timid in childhood, Clara Barton grew up to be a famous nurse and founder of the American Red Cross Society.

cated would affect not only Clara herself, but all those whom Clara would help throughout her life. Stephen and Sarah Barton were strict, hardworking parents, but their household was a liberal one for the time.

Clara spent most of her spare time with her brothers, from whom she learned to ride horses and play ball games. It was during this active, tomboyish childhood that Clara became comfortable in the company of males.

When Clara was 10, her brother David was injured in an accidental fall. Clara appointed herself David's nurse and cared for him for nearly two years. She was a constant companion to the bedridden young man until she was 13.

It seemed as though Clara needed to be needed—otherwise she felt unfocused, even useless. Throughout her life this proved to be the case, although Clara would have little trouble finding causes worthy of her boundless energy.

Clara and her oldest brother, Stephen—who would later be superintendent of schools in his hometown—successfully lobbied for a public school system that would accept poor boys and girls and be paid for by taxpayers, rather than by parents. In the 1840s, such a system was new and extremely modern. It took several years for the town government to agree.

A few years later Clara accepted an invitation from a friend, Mary Norton, to stay with the Nortons in Hightstown, New Jersey. Just as in Massachusetts years before, Clara found the school system in Hightstown somewhat backwards and certainly inadequate. Shocked to find that there was no school for children of parents who could not afford to pay tuition, Clara began a one-woman campaign to found a free school in Bordentown, New Jersey. She agreed to teach without pay, provided the community would offer a building and adequate materials.

Her project was successful—so successful that the town decided the school was too big to be run by a woman. Clara resigned, furious. She and her friend Fanny Childs, who had come to Bordentown to help Clara with her growing school, decided to move to Washington, D.C. Clara was ready to give up teaching, and in 1854 she set off for the nation's capital, where she found work as a clerk for the Patent Office. Judge Charles Mason, the head of the Patent Office, supported her and other female clerks when outside pressure urged him to fire them and hire men. Mason was particularly supportive of Clara, who assisted his efforts to root out fraud and corruption in government offices.

But Mason's job was an appointed one, and after James Buchanan's election to the presidency in 1856, he lost influence. Clara returned to North Oxford in 1857 but kept up her connections in Washington and sought a suitable job. Few employers, however, would hire a woman, even a talented one. Finally, in 1860, Clara was asked to return to a job at the Patent Office, at a lower pay.

The political events that led to the Civil War unfolded over the next few months. Then came President Lincoln's call for volunteers to preserve the Union. Raw recruits flooded the capital, and the government was ill-prepared to help them. Clara knew that there would soon be bloodshed, and that she must help.

Clara bought food, clothing, soap, and other supplies and asked for donations from everyone she knew. When Massachusetts volunteers were injured in riots of angry southerners in Baltimore, Clara wrote to friends in Massachusetts, asking them to send supplies. She used her own savings and earn-

This 1884 engraving depicts the "Angel of the Battlefield" at Strasbourg with the conquering Prussian army in 1870.

ings as a clerk for the next several years; perhaps more importantly, she used her connections and her gift of persuasion to get others to help as well.

As the war intensified and Clara continued to donate supplies, she heard wounded soldiers describe the conditions on the battlefields. There were never enough doctors or nurses, never enough medicine or bandages, and the wounded lay for hours—even days—before any help arrived. There weren't even enough people to distribute water and food to the men; the army just was not organized enough to provide adequate care.

Clara knew that a proper lady would never try to serve on a battlefield. She also knew that she had to help. She spent about a year trying to persuade government officials to let her go to the front lines, where she could help the most. Meanwhile she continued to write to soldiers' families, who then sent whatever supplies they could: soap, clothing, bandages, food.

In 1862 Clara received a military pass. She loaded a wagon and drove toward the front, finally arriving at Cedar Mountain, Virginia. Here Clara earned her nickname, "Angel of the Battlefield," when a hard-pressed army surgeon wrote his wife of Clara's unexpected arrival, just as he had run out of bandages.

Clara and three female volunteers hopped on a train when news arrived of the massive battle near Bull Run, Virginia. And so she continued throughout the war, serving independently of aid societies like the Sanitary Commission, and independently of any government agency. Clara was fearless when serving others. At times, as she stepped between the wounded on the ground, her skirt grew heavy with blood. Other times bullets just missed her, leaving holes in her clothing. Sometimes Clara performed duties more suitable to surgeons (who were always male). Once, for example, she cut a man's cheek open, at his request, to remove a bullet. Few had any words but praise for the small lady with endless energy. She became more and more famous as newspapers printed accounts of her actions.

After the war, family members of missing soldiers wrote desperate letters to the famous nurse, hoping she might remember nursing their loved ones. There was little she could do, but her heart went out to these families. Clara yet again decided to take action. She compiled lists of the missing men's names and had them published in dozens of newspapers, asking readers to help find out where the men were, or what had happened to them. Again using her own money, Clara located over 22,000 missing men by 1869.

While visiting England and Scotland in 1869 to rest after a lecture tour, Clara met Dr. Louis Appia in Geneva, Switzerland. Appia described to her the organization known as the Red Cross. When several nations signed the Treaty of Geneva in 1864, the Red Cross was formed to train medical assistants who would serve the soldiers of any nation during wartime. To prevent their being fired upon by either side in a conflict, the volunteers would display a badge of a red cross on a white background, which is where the group got its name. The United States had not yet signed the treaty, and Appia sought the famous woman's help.

When the Franco-Prussian war broke out in 1870, Clara was enthusiastic to help the victims of the battles. For the most part the work was difficult and dangerous. The Red Cross was not yet well-known or respected by either soldiers or civilians. Soon the women gained the support of influential people, like Louise, Grand Duchess of Baden. With the help of these powerful people, Clara and her assistants were

Barton inspects a Red Cross orphanage in Cuba in 1899, after the Spanish-American War.

able to direct supplies to where they were most needed.

Clara decided to return to the United States in 1874, where she hoped that her health would improve with rest. During her long convalescence at a hospital in New York state, she wrote letters to Dr. Louis Appia asking about the Red Cross's progress in Europe. Because the United States decided not to sign the Geneva Treaty, it would not be affiliated with the International Red Cross.

Clara, however, was as determined as ever to help others. In 1881 she formed the American Red Cross Society. Her organization was not an official branch of the Red Cross, but it was modeled after its European counterpart. In addition to aiding victims of war, the American Red Cross Society sought to help victims of natural disasters like floods, hurricanes, tornadoes, earthquakes, and fires. A few months later, when forest fires ravaged Michigan, the society sent supplies worth about $80,000.

Throughout the next several years, Clara kept very busy. One of the biggest disasters occurred in Johnstown, Pennsylvania, in 1889, when a dam burst and the entire town flooded within minutes. As soon as a train could get through, Clara Barton arrived. She and other Red Cross Society workers stayed for five months, helping to care for the survivors and clean up the town. The American Red Cross Society also helped the victims of an 1893 hurricane in South Carolina, which hit the Sea Islands particularly hard, and the 1900 hurricane that struck Galveston, Texas. Clara's idea that the Red Cross Society should help victims of disasters as well as of war was later adopted by the International Red Cross too.

After trips to Europe, Turkey, and Cuba to attend conferences and help victims of war, Clara began to be criticized by some American Red Cross Society volunteers. The organization, like Clara's earlier activities, centered around her. Clara was the president, appointed for life, of the national organization. Eager to be in the middle of the action, she rushed off to battle lines and disaster areas, and that left no one to perform the administrative duties that would make the organization larger and stronger. Local branch leaders began to wonder why the national society, frequently accused of unfair practices, was not required to answer to anyone.

Clara herself was hurt and appalled by the suggestions of wrongdoing and the criticism she received. She was even accused of pilfering Red Cross Society funds for herself. The charges had little or no foundation. Clara Barton routinely spent her own money, and solicited thousands of dollars from donors, on the causes she was engaged in. A 1904 investigation completely cleared Clara's name, but the controversy hurt the organization. Clara finally decided to resign her presidency and retire.

In retirement, though, Clara kept active. She served as honorary president of the National First Aid Association of America, supported women's suffrage, and wrote an account of her childhood. In 1908 she injured her back and never fully recovered, although her mental faculties never dulled. She died at age 90 in April 1912.

In old age Barton continued to be active in social causes.

MARIE CURIE

$\mathbf{M}$arie Curie has become one of the most recognizable names in the field of physics and chemistry. Because of her well-known husband, Pierre Curie, she is often associated with France. But Maria Sklodowska born in Warsaw, Poland, in 1867, during a time when the Poles were subject to brutal repression by the tzarist regime of Russia.

Maria's parents, Bronislawa and Wladyslaw, married in 1860, and her mother became headmistress of a prestigious girls' school that same year. While she was working at this post, Bronislawa bore five children: Zofia, Jozef, Bronislawa (called Bronia), Helena, and Maria. Their parents were both well educated and descended from nobility, but they had lost their lands and fortunes in fighting the Russian takeover. Wladyslaw became a teacher and struggled against the Russian government's regulation of education. Laws forbade young Polish schoolchildren from learning in Polish and forced them to learn Polish history as seen by the conquering Russians.

Wladyslaw was assistant director of a government-run

Marie Curie in 1898, the year she and her husband discovered radium.

school called a gymnasium from 1868 to 1873. Bright, curious, disciplined, and a natural teacher, Wladyslaw delighted in teaching his children everything he knew.

Girls generally did not attend gymnasia; more often they went to private schools like the one Branislaw directed. She quit her job when Wladyslaw was hired at the gymnasium and devoted her time to teaching her children at home. Together the parents provided a rigorous education for their children, in spite of the limitations placed on Polish schools and educators.

Shortly after her mother's death Maria was placed in a gymnasium. Jozef, Bronia, and Maria all graduated from gymnasium at the head of each of their classes—Maria in 1883, at the early age of 15. Unlike Jozef, however, Maria and her sisters were not allowed to enroll in Warsaw University. Instead, the three daughters studied at home, tutoring students to bring in money. None, apparently, wished to marry; all hoped to attend university, despite their poverty. Maria and Bronia took classes at a secret "university" that met wherever it could—often in people's homes.

After a year, Maria took a job as a governess. After another year she quit and took a new post in the countryside. Maria agreed to help send Bronia to study in Paris; when Bronia finished school she could help support Maria's studies.

In 1888 Maria seems to have been in love with the eldest son of her employers, who was a year older than she. The parents blocked a marriage, however, thinking Maria too poor, and the son eventually rejected her. Finally, she saved enough to go to university.

The next few years were filled with hard but fulfilling work. The only fees at the Sorbonne, her university, were charged for licenses or diplomas—not for classes. So Marie, as she was now called, could attend as many classes as she wanted. Her only social life, she later said, was discussing scientific problems with classmates. Nevertheless, she was as happy as she had ever been. She was frustrated only by her lack of laboratory space.

In 1893 she received her degree in physics; she had planned, after this, to return to Warsaw to care for her father and become a teacher. However, a friend arranged a large scholarship for her, and she returned to Paris. In 1894 she received her second degree, in mathematics, again intending to return to Warsaw. That spring, however, she had met Pierre Curie, eight years her elder. He was a scientist at the City School of Physics and Industrial Chemistry—a less prestigious school, certainly, than the Sorbonne. A mutual friend introduced the two in the hope that Marie would be allowed access to better laboratory space.

Marie and Pierre Curie stand in the garden of their Paris home with their daughter Irene.

Although both Pierre and Marie had been hurt in romance before and were reluctant to involve themselves again, they fell in love quickly. Pierre had worked for years without bothering to obtain an official diploma. Now he received his degree and won a professorship at the City School, they married in July 1895.

In September 1897, Marie gave birth to their first

daughter, Irene. Around the same time, Marie decided to begin work on her doctoral thesis. She was interested in studying the strange rays that emanated from compounds that included the element uranium. In 1896 Henri Becquerel had discovered this property, but most scientists of the time were focused on other work—including electricity. It was left to Marie Curie to explain and name the phenomenon that Becquerel had observed: radioactivity.

Marie worked in a drafty, ill-supplied room in the basement of her husband's school, when she could make time away from teaching. Although it was her project, Pierre often worked with her, as the two were rarely separated, particularly in their scientific work. The couple built their own equipment to test the rays, if any, given off by pure elements.

One day in 1898, Marie tested pitchblende, which was a black compound containing uranium. It gave off rays stronger than those of uranium alone. She tested other compounds containing uranium, but these gave off fewer, less powerful rays than uranium alone. And another element, thorium, also emitted these strange rays. In December 1898, the Curies isolated and named this ray-giving substance: radium.

For the next several years, Marie devoted herself to measuring the atomic weight of radium, so that it could be added to the periodic table of the elements. She finished this task in 1902; meanwhile Pierre studied radioactive properties. This, too, was one of the happiest times in Marie's life; she and Pierre worked together, utterly absorbed in their work as if in a dream. Income came, happily, from awards, prizes, and publication of their work.

At the time, scientists could not know that the same quality that made radium products glow also caused radiation burns and serious illnesses like can-

cer. Eventually both Curies would become ill, but they simply thought they were working too hard.

In 1903 came the news that Marie and Pierre Curie were to share with Henri Becquerel one of the most prestigious awards in the world: the Nobel Prize in physics.

It was something of a struggle to see that Marie was given the recognition she deserved: at first, the nomination included only Pierre. Marie was the only woman to be awarded a Nobel Prize for science, until her own daughter won the Nobel Prize in 1935. Many people at the time were so surprised by the idea that a married couple worked together as equals that they assumed that Marie was simply Pierre's assistant.

As for Pierre, sixteen months after the Nobel Prize was announced, he was finally elected a member of the prestigious Academy of Science. He also began teaching classes at the Sorbonne.

Their second daughter, Eve, was born in December 1905, but Marie continued to teach at a girls' school. She enjoyed getting young women excited over the study of physics and mathematics, and she earned a reputation for being a teacher whose students stayed after the bell, so interested in what they were learning that they didn't want to leave.

In April 1906, disaster struck. Pierre, hurrying across a traffic-filled street in Paris, was struck by a large wagon and died instantly. Marie was inconsolable. After several months she was able to return to her experiments, gradually. Amazingly, the Sorbonne offered the chair of chemistry that had been created for Pierre to Marie. She accepted, to continue his work in his memory. Meanwhile, Marie obtained funding from the University of Paris and other prestigious organizations to build a laboratory to be known as the Radium Institute.

Curie with her daughter Eve in the early 1920s.

In 1921 Curie is honored by U.S. President Warren G. Harding with the gift of a tube of radium.

In 1910 Marie was nominated for admission to the Academy of Science; after a hugely controversial debate, with feminists and scientists arguing for her election and conservatives and other scientists arguing that women should not be admitted, Marie lost by two votes.

At the end of that year, Marie was awarded the Nobel Prize again, this time for chemistry. In the years between her first award and this one, scientists were making more and more discoveries about the properties of radioactivity, and the uses to which it could be applied. It was thought, for example, that eventually a cure or treatment for cancer could be developed from it. Marie's discovery and isolation of radium had created a whole new field of science, and it was for this discovery, made years before, that she was honored with her second Nobel Prize.

Shortly after the outbreak of World War I in 1914, Marie found a way to contribute to the French war effort, and put to silence forever the lingering doubts on "the foreign woman's" love for her adopted country. In addition to buying French war bonds with most of her Nobel Prize money, Marie developed a number of radiology cars for use by the French army. Marie opposed war but did not involve herself in political issues, feeling that the best way she could contribute was through science. She used equipment that lay unused in laboratories to construct X-ray machines, then had them mounted to motor cars so they could be transported to front-line hospitals. The machines could be used with the electricity generated by the car's motor, or using electricity, if available, at the hospital itself. Her daughter Irene also helped the war effort, at the same time she earned degrees from the Sorbonne in math, physics, and chemistry.

After the war, Marie successfully campaigned for

Irene's appointment as a laboratory assistant at the Radium Institute. Until Marie's death in 1934, her daughter assisted her as well as conducting her own experiments (she also won the Nobel Prize in chemistry in 1935, with her husband Frederick Joliot).

In her later years, Marie devoted most of her time to directing her laboratory assistants, a remarkable proportion of whom were foreigners and women. Meanwhile, the Radium Institute and the Pasteur Institute (which had helped fund Marie's laboratory) were winning valuable grants and fellowships that enabled them to grow and join with other scientific institutions. Eventually these bodies became the National Center of Scientific Research, an organization that was to win a great deal of the prestige that had in the past been given to the Academy.

Also during these years, the results of long exposure to radioactivity were becoming more and more obvious. Scientists began to learn that the amounts of radiation they thought were acceptable were actually incredibly dangerous. Marie herself was apparently particularly resistant to radiation sickness, but even she suffered numerous complaints such as scarred fingers from radium burns, and advanced anemia—a condition of the blood that prevents oxygen absorption and causes intense fatigue.

Marie spent the last few years of her life with her daughters and new grandchildren (Irene and Frederick had two children), and visiting friends and her brothers and sisters. In July 1934 she died; Jozef and Bronia both came to the funeral with small containers of Polish soil, which they sprinkled on her coffin. Marie was buried next to her beloved Pierre.

MARGARET MEAD

4

Margaret Mead believed strongly that the way she was raised directly influenced her choice of career and her success at it. Her parents taught her, she said, to observe and take interest in the world and people around her. Now, her name is forever linked with the study of native peoples of the Pacific islands. In addition, she did not hesitate to speak her own opinions on American culture during a century in which it was rapidly changing.

Born in 1901, Margaret was the eldest of the five children (one died while still a baby) of Emily Fogg Mead and Edward Sherwood Mead. Her mother, a vibrantly intelligent and socially conscious woman, earned a Ph.D. in sociology. Her father was an economist who taught at the prestigious Wharton School of Business at the University of Pennsylvania, edited a magazine, and wrote several books.

Mead herself credited her father's mother, Martha Ramsey Mead, with instilling in her a deep respect for tradition as well as a healthy individuality. This grandmother was a very liberated woman who encouraged Margaret to remain

Encouraged by her parents and grandmother, Margaret Mead became a strong individual and a pioneering anthropologist.

Margaret and her brother, Richard, in 1911.

true to her own strong personality. She was almost the only teacher of Margaret, her two sisters, and one brother. One biographer states that "while other grade-school children were spelling three-letter words, [the Mead children] were studying botany and algebra." This somewhat haphazard style of education was supplemented by tutors hired by their mother, Emily. The combined effect on Margaret was a devotion to the value of interdisciplinary study. That is, she did not limit herself to the knowledge found in one field, but combined knowledge from different fields.

It could be said that Margaret began her fieldwork when her mother gave her a notebook for recording the milestones of her baby sisters. Young Margaret became fascinated by the task and continued this kind of recording for her whole life, with her own daughter as well as the people she studied.

The Mead children were not taught a specific religion, but at age 11 Margaret chose to join the Episcopal church. She attended De Pauw University in Chicago in 1919, but such a freethinker was not welcome in the social atmosphere of fraternities and sororities. During this year she became engaged to Luther Cressman, who was studying to be an Episcopal minister. Her year at

De Pauw convinced her that coeducation (males and females together) was not good for bright women, because they did not receive enough encouragement despite doing better, on the whole, than bright men did. Margaret went to Barnard College in New York City instead, in 1920. In 1923 she received her bachelor's degree, and that autumn she and Cressman married. Mead kept her own name.

After Mead received her master's degree in psychology from Columbia University in 1924, she went on to study with notable anthropologists Franz Boas and Ruth Benedict. Benedict became a particularly close friend. Partly from their influence, and partly because of her father's belief that "the most important thing anyone could do was to add to the world's store of knowledge," Margaret chose to study social science, specifically anthropology.

She and Cressman were happy for a time, but when Mead had almost finished her doctoral dissertation in psychology at Columbia University, she decided to do fieldwork in Polynesia. Cressman, meanwhile, wanted to study in Europe. Margaret received a fellowship—partly because her parents were financially as well as morally supportive—and set out for Samoa in 1925. Hers was a dangerous mission at a time when women were actively discouraged from conducting fieldwork. Many anthropologists then did not consider fieldwork necessary and focused their research instead on artifacts and cultural collections in major museums. Boaz himself was reluctant to let the petite Mead go to the South Seas, an area that was known for its cannibals and for tropical diseases that had already killed several anthropologists. Samoa was chosen partly because a ship stopped there regularly, and Margaret's safety could be checked on.

Mead's task was made more difficult by her lack

Mead displays a wooden artifact in 1928, the year of her second field trip.

of practical experience. She had enough book learning, but had yet to learn how to use equipment and how to protect her possessions in tropical humidity. She also needed to shed the "cultural baggage" of her own background so that she could do her work well without becoming so involved with Samoans that she could not study them objectively. Mead developed methods by trial and error. Not only was she the first anthropologist to study many of the people she visited, but she later became one of the first teachers of field methods as well.

Mead's nine months of study in Samoa were detailed in her best-selling book *Coming of Age in Samoa*, published in 1928. In Samoa, she found, the maturity of young men and women was not a period fraught with tension and rebellion, as it was in Western civilizations. The book showed that the problems associated with adolescence in Western societies were shaped by culture and customs, not by the physical changes of adolescence.

Upon her return, Margaret was told by a doctor that she could not have children. Luther, meanwhile, had left the ministry and become a sociologist. She and Luther agreed to divorce. Both of their lives and plans had changed so much that they felt they had little in common any longer. This matter-of-fact approach to marriage, although sensible in light of Margaret's chosen career, was quite radical at the time, and still is to many people. Margaret stands out for being a woman who did not feel that any of her three marriages were failures: she believed that each marriage simply ran its course.

Mead's second field trip, in 1928, was with her second husband, New Zealand–born anthropologist Reo Fortune, to study the Manus people of the Admiralty Islands. The two returned to New York, where they worked together and separately to pub-

In 1957 Mead returns for a brief visit to Bali, where she and Gregory Bateson conducted a two-year study in the 1930s.

lish books based on their research. Margaret's book *Sex and Temperament in Three Primitive Societies* (1935) was one of her most famous; it chronicled the gender roles in three very different cultures and showed that what Americans assume are "feminine" or "masculine" traits are actually based on culture, not biological difference. Margaret received her Ph.D. from Columbia University in 1929.

Mead's professional collaboration with Reo Fortune lasted about five years. She studied several different tribes during this time and said later that fieldwork with Fortune, since he was a man, enabled her to get a more complete picture of the cultures she studied than she would have gotten by herself. But by about 1935 the independent Mead felt it was "fatiguing to be constantly boosting [Fortune's] ego," and Fortune himself found it difficult to stay married to the unique and forceful Mead. They divorced in 1935. The next year, Mead married another anthropologist, Englishman Gregory Bateson, with whom she and Fortune had worked in New Guinea.

In 1936 Mead and Bateson traveled to Bali, where

they spent two years using a camera to document Balinese culture. (In 1941 their book *Balinese Character: A Photographic Analysis* was published.) Margaret said in her 1972 autobiography, *Blackberry Winter*, that this was probably the happiest period of her life. In 1939 they returned to New York, where despite having had several miscarriages, Mead gave birth to Bateson's daughter, Mary Catherine. Mary Catherine grew up much like Margaret herself had: in a variety of different places, but always surrounded by caring and nurturing people, who treated her more as an independent human than as an inexperienced child. Margaret and Mary Catherine lived mostly in Philadelphia and New York, while Bateson himself, particularly during World War II, worked mostly in England. Eventually the couple grew apart, and the marriage ended by about 1950. The rest of Mead's life was spent as a single woman, collaborating with a number of professional colleagues.

Although Mead cut back on her field study so she could care for her daughter, she continued her career by studying American culture and habits. She kept her job, which she had held since 1927, of assistant curator of ethnology at the American Museum of Natural History in New York; she also continued writing books and articles. From 1934 until her death, she taught at Columbia University. She founded the Institute for Intercultural Studies at the museum in 1944. She served on a number of committees and research groups, including a study of American food habits for the National Research Council; the National Institute for Mental Health; and the World Federation for Mental Health. She was an eminent and sought-after lecturer during these years as well.

Mead's only major field trip after her daughter's birth was in 1953. She returned to the village of Peri, where she had studied the Manus in 1928–29. She had heard of the immense changes in the Manus' culture since they had come in contact with Western societies during World War II, and she was anxious to document the changes as they were still occurring.

In the 1970s, Mead's Hall of the Peoples of the Pacific was completed at the American Museum of Natural History. This wing of the museum chronicled Mead's own life's work, showing the development in the 20th century of peoples, Margaret herself said, "who stepped straight from the Stone Age into an airplane with virtually nothing in between." Mead believed strongly that anthropologists have a responsibility to the people they study—a responsibility to serve as cultural interpreters to governments who intrude on "Stone Age" societies, to prevent unnecessary upheaval in village life and beliefs.

Mead wrote a monthly column in the popular women's magazine *Redbook* from 1961 to 1978. Her views on the family, urbanization, women's rights, sexuality, and other moral and social issues were, like Margaret herself, outspoken and radical for the time. Her attitudes and public support of the women's movement in America stemmed from her own experiences as a child as well as from her astute observations of other cultures. She believed that the social sciences and particularly anthropology should make themselves useful to society. They should apply their knowledge to public policy to solve the dilemmas of modern life. She died in New York City of cancer in 1978, undoubtedly the best known anthropologist of all time.

RACHEL CARSON

Rachel Carson knew from a very young age that she wanted to be a writer. Her first short story was published in *St. Nicholas,* a children's magazine, in 1918; she was 10 years old when she wrote it. Since then, the magazine printed several more stories of hers, but this summer day in 1921 was the first time they had paid her for her work: one cent per word. By getting her literary start in *St. Nicholas* magazine, Rachel joined some illustrious company. William Faulkner, F. Scott Fitzgerald, E. B. White, the poet e. e. cummings, Edna St. Vincent Millay—all were first published in *St. Nicholas.*

Besides reading and writing, Rachel loved being outdoors. She and her mother shared an intense interest in wildlife—plants, animals, anything. Her mother, Maria, had been a schoolteacher and a musician before she married her husband, Robert, in 1894. Maria already had two other children, Robert and Marian, but both of them were in school by the time Rachel was born. Maria could spend long hours teaching her baby daughter all about nature, and encourag-

Rachel Carson pursued a career that combined her two loves: writing and studying nature.

ing her to read and make up stories herself. Rachel became a good student.

Rachel spent most of her childhood outside, but she also read lots of books about nature. She became fascinated by the ocean when she found fossilized shells near her home in Springfield, Pennsylvania, and wondered what kinds of animals had lived in them and what happened to the ocean they lived in.

Robert Carson Sr. spent a lot of time traveling, struggling to make a living selling insurance. Rachel's family was not wealthy at all and lived some distance from the town center. This made it hard for her to keep up friendships with other children, but Rachel wasn't lonely. Her mother was a constant teacher and friend, and the two would rarely be separated. Maria encouraged her daughter to study hard; she planned a different life for her youngest child than the life her older children were leading. Like their father, they struggled to make enough to support their families.

Maria wanted Rachel to study hard, so she could one day support herself, whether she chose to marry or not. Rachel, too, saw Maria's troubles, and besides, she loved the world of ideas and writing. When she went away to Pittsburgh to attend the Pennsylvania College for Women (now called Chatham College), she wanted to study English and be a writer.

Instead, after taking a required biology course, Rachel followed her love of nature, going against some teachers' and friends' advice, and changed her major to biology. At the time, the sciences were considered men's work, and there were very few women who made a living in science. One of them, Mary Scott Skinker, was Rachel's teacher. She became one of Rachel's closest lifelong friends and her professional mentor. Rachel received her bachelor's degree in biology magna cum laude (with great honors) in 1929. She was one of only three students in her class to receive such honors.

In 1929 and for a few years afterwards, Rachel spent her summers at the Woods Hole Marine Biological Lab in Massachusetts. That first summer, she won a scholarship to study there. She also won a scholarship to study zoology at Johns Hopkins University in Baltimore, and she moved there in the fall. Maria and Rachel missed each other and could not afford to pay for visits or even phone calls at such a distance. And by now, Rachel's mother, father, sister, and nieces were dependent on Rachel's contributions to the family income. They moved to nearby Stemmers Run, Maryland in 1930.

Two years later Rachel earned her master's degree in zoology. She began doctoral studies right away and taught classes at Johns Hopkins and at the University of Maryland to help make ends meet. On the Carson family, which had never been well-off, the Great Depression was taking its toll. Rachel dropped out of her studies in 1934 to find a more regular job than part-time teaching.

During her search for a job as a scientist with the U.S. government, Rachel found a part-time job that let her combine her love of science with her talent at writing. She wrote several radio scripts for the U.S. Bureau of Fisheries (later called the U.S. Fish and Wildlife Service). During this temporary job, Mary Scott Skinker helped her study for the civil service exam, so that Rachel would be eligible for a research position when one came open. She scored very high and was soon hired as a junior aquatic biologist.

In 1937, Rachel sold her first major story, "Undersea," to the *Atlantic Monthly*. She was not paid very

Although science was considered men's work at the time, Carson won scholarships to study biology.

much, but she would from then on be recognized as someone who could make scientific subjects interesting and enjoyable to nonscientists.

Carson kept writing at night and on weekends, about the ocean in particular. She had several more articles published in the late 1930s. Although she originally thought that she had to give up writing when she chose biology, she said later that "it never occurred to me that I was merely getting something to write about."

Finally, in late 1941, Carson's first book was published. *Under the Sea-Wind* examined the wildlife that lived alongside or above, rather than underneath, the world's oceans. The book did not sell very well.

Throughout the 1940s Carson concentrated on her full-time job and on caring for her family. During the war, Carson wrote conservation bulletins for other government agencies. Afterwards, she was responsible for a series of illustrated booklets about the national wildlife refuges. The booklets were not, if Carson's literary style had anything to do with it, typical government publications. In 1949, she was promoted to editor in chief.

That same year, the writing bug bit Rachel again. She began the research for another book, *The Sea Around Us*, which was published in 1951. It was such a huge hit that Carson quit her job the following year so she could write full-time. *The Sea Around Us* stayed on the *New York Times* bestseller list for 86 weeks—a year and a half—and won the National Book Award. Carson appeared on television, and a documentary film of her book—even though it was filled with mistakes that bothered Carson—won an Academy Award. Despite all the sudden exposure, Carson remained shy and private, saying that the career of a writer required solitude.

The book was so successful that the earlier work *Under the Sea-Wind* was reissued in 1952. It, too, finally enjoyed success, and with the income from both books, Carson had an income she could count on. Now she could devote all of her time to writing—and she was, by her own admission, a slow writer. She preferred to research very carefully, and she revised almost up until the minute the piece was published. She revised sentence by sentence, paragraph by paragraph. She went through dozens of drafts for even a short article, and to her nothing was complete until it read well out loud as well as on the page.

Carson moved to an out-of-the-way coastal cottage in Maine to research her next book. After three years, *The Edge of the Sea* was published in 1955. This book was also a best-seller that won numerous awards, and Carson was elected to the prestigious and exclusive American Academy of Arts and Letters (it had only 50 members). *The Edge of the Sea* examined the life that teems on the seashore, and like Carson's other books, it viewed the environment as something to which humans belong, not something which they master. With this book, Carson tried (and succeeded) "to take the seashore out of the category of scenery and make it come alive."

Carson followed the controversy surrounding the increasing use of pesticides in the 1940s and 1950s, particularly one called DDT. She began actively researching pesticides in the late 1950s and tried to sell articles on the subject. Editors thought the subject was too dark. But Carson felt the subject was something that *must* be addressed; she was angry about what she knew was happening to the environment. She persisted with her topic. Finally, after four years of research, she published her most famous book, *Silent Spring*, in 1962. The book was

Carson (right) attends a 1962 women's conference in New York, with Assistant Secretary of Labor Esther Peterson (left) and Mrs. Varnall Jacobs, president of the National Council of Women.

enormously popular, but it generated fierce criticism from industrialists, who tried to portray Carson as a "hysterical woman" rather than an intelligent scientist with hard evidence. As a result of the controversy, the Kennedy administration's Science Advisory Committee looked into the pesticide situation. The committee found that Carson was right and the industrialists were wrong. The committee's report, in turn, sparked activity in state governments: By the end of 1963, more than 40 bills had been introduced in state legislatures to regulate pesticides. *Silent Spring* helped launch the environmental movement in America.

Rachel Carson was diagnosed with cancer in 1960. She suffered also from an ulcer, arthritis, and heart disease. None of these health problems stopped her from appearing, as late as 1963, before Congress to urge the government to control pesticide use before it was too late. But her health worsened, and Rachel Carson died in April 1964, a few weeks before her 57th birthday.

In 1965, *A Sense of Wonder* was published, based on an article Rachel had written about teaching children to love the natural world. It had been inspired by her great-nephew Roger, whom she had adopted after his mother died. And in 1969, the wildlife refuge near her cottage in Maine was renamed the Rachel Carson Natural Wildlife Refuge. Finally, in 1980, Rachel Carson was posthumously awarded the highest American civilian award, the Presidential Medal of Freedom.

ANTONIA NOVELLO

One day in 1960, a teenage girl ran down the stairs at her school. She was excited, looking for her friends to tell them the good news: she had gotten an A from a teacher who never gave them. Before she found her friends, she heard them talking—about *her*. They were saying that she would get an A just because her mother was the principal. Her mother would make sure that all the teachers gave her daughter good grades, they thought. They didn't think the girl's good grades were her own.

The girl was Antonia Coello. She decided then, as a junior in high school, that she would try even harder to have perfect grades. "I studied so hard that I took the entry examination to college in my junior year"—because in case she failed, she would have another year to study for it and take it again. But Antonia didn't fail. "To my surprise, I had the highest grade in the school."

By this time Antonia had already thought she wanted to be a doctor. She knew it would be hard—she was a poor girl, and she had an illness that needed surgery to cure. It was a

Antonia Novello speaks out as the first female surgeon general of the United States.

big dream. But even Antonia never dreamed that she would be the first woman surgeon general of the United States.

Antonia, called "Tonita" when she was little, was born in Fajardo, Puerto Rico, in 1944. Antonia's family was poor. Her mother was a schoolteacher, and when Antonia was very young her parents divorced.

Antonia was born with an illness called congenital megacolon. The colon, part of the large intestine, helps digest food after the stomach and small intestine have broken it down. Antonia says that having no nerve cells in her colon meant that she "was born without the cells that make you think you have to go to the bathroom." Antonia's colon would swell painfully. Every summer she went to a hospital for several weeks for treatment, and the swelling would go away. Antonia remembers thinking when she was very young that she wanted to be a doctor too, so she could help other sick children.

Antonia studied hard and joined many clubs at school. She didn't want people to think that her sickness made her unable to do everything they could do. Her mother told her over and over that she was "not going to let your disease be used for you not to succeed." Antonia knew her mother expected the best from her, whether she was sick or well. She learned to overlook her illness and "act like nothing was wrong"—and, after all, nothing really was: her mind still worked.

Antonia graduated from high school in 1961 and went to the University of Puerto Rico at Rio Piedras. During her college years Antonia had her first operation. Healing took a long time, and she had to wear diapers to class. From this Antonia learned to laugh at herself, because wearing diapers made it particularly hard to pretend nothing was wrong! In 1964

Antonia went, by herself, to a hospital in Minnesota, thousands of miles away. She had to have another operation. Still, despite all this, she kept up the hard work to earn her bachelor of science degree in 1965.

Antonia's illness was cured by the time she was 20, but she lived with it long enough to remember what it's like to be sick. And she believes that having a health problem is not an excuse to stop working hard. "You can be sick and get to the top, absolutely," she says. "Don't get disappointed because sickness puts you down. . . . People will always help you." Antonia herself became one of the people who help.

Antonia waited until she was accepted into medical school to tell her mother. She didn't want her mother to be disappointed if she wasn't accepted. Both women were very excited. But that year, Antonia's aunt died of a kidney disease. The disease was treatable, but the doctors who saw her were not specialists. So when Antonia went to medical school she decided to study kidney diseases, an area of specialization called nephrology. She still wanted to help children, so she also studied pediatrics. Finally she earned her medical degree in 1970 from the University of Puerto Rico at San Juan, a bigger city than Rio Piedras.

The day after graduation, Antonia married Joseph Novello, a man she had met in medical school. He was in the U.S. Navy and stationed in Puerto Rico. He later became a flight surgeon. The Novellos then moved to Ann Arbor, Michigan, to continue their studies.

Antonia worked at the University of Michigan Medical Center as an intern, and then as a resident doctor, until 1974. One year, she won the Intern of the Year Award. She was considered the most car-

In 1990 Novello is sworn in as surgeon general as her husband, Dr. Joseph Novello, holds the Bible. Supreme Court Justice Sandra Day O'Connor administers the oath while President George Bush looks on.

ing and hard-working intern in the pediatric department at the medical center. It was the first time a woman had won the award.

In 1974, Antonia received a fellowship to study at Georgetown University, and the Novellos moved to Washington, D.C. Here, Antonia worked as a professor of pediatrics in the university medical center. Then she set up a private practice as a pediatrician. But seeing so many children who were seriously ill made her very sad. "When the pediatrician cries as much as the parents do, then you know it's time to get out," she said.

So she got out and went to work for the U.S. Public Health Service. This organization educates the public about health problems and illness prevention; it also sends doctors to areas where there is a shortage of physicians. Antonia still helped people, but now she helped people stay well.

She also served as an advisor to the U.S. government, helping to draft legislation. Some of the laws she helped with dealt with warning labels on cigarette packages, and regulated organ donation. To gain knowledge that would help her do this job even better, Antonia received a master's degree in public health from Johns Hopkins University in Baltimore, in 1982.

In 1979, Antonia joined the National Institutes of Health. She worked with the Institute of Arthritis, Metabolism, and Digestive Diseases and finally became, in 1986, the deputy director of the Institute of Child Health and Human Development. In this job she focused her energy on pediatric AIDS.

AIDS, or Acquired Immune Deficiency Syndrome, is a disease caused by a virus called HIV (Human Immunodeficiency Virus); there is no cure for AIDS. It was discovered in the 1980s, and Antonia was especially concerned about children who have the disease. She brought public attention to the fact that pregnant women with AIDS or with HIV pass the disease on to their babies. Antonia was interested in laws affecting these children, and AIDS patients in general. She thought the government needed to spend more money on researchers who are trying to find a cure.

Soon she caught the attention of President George Bush, who was elected in 1988. In 1989, Bush nominated her to be the next surgeon general, and Congress approved the nomination. In early 1990, Antonia was sworn in. She was the first woman, and the first Latin American, to become surgeon general.

In 1992 Novello demanded that Camel cigarettes stop using "Joe Camel" in advertising campaigns. The cartoon character, she argued, helped convince young people to take up smoking.

The surgeon general is the head of the U.S. Public Health Service. He or she is, in theory, the doctor for all Americans; he or she holds a military rank and wears a military uniform. It's an important job—for Antonia it was especially important. She wanted to be a role model for women and for minorities. Her first public appearance as surgeon general was in Puerto Rico. "When I got off the plane," she said, "kids from my mother's school lined both sides of the road handing me flowers. I went to the [veterans'] hospital to speak. When the veterans saw my gold braid they all stood and saluted . . . I realized that for these people, for women, I have to be good as a doctor, I have to be good as a surgeon general, I have to be everything."

While she was surgeon general, Antonia worked hard to educate people about important health issues like smoking, underage drinking, and AIDS. She criticized tobacco companies and beer and liquor companies for targeting their advertising to teenagers and even younger kids. She called attention to domestic violence. She also spoke out about health issues that affect the Hispanic community and women and children in particular.

In 1993 Antonia left the job of surgeon general to work with UNICEF. UNICEF is the United Nations' children's health fund. She was the special representative for health and nutrition until 1996. In this job Antonia helped children all over the world: many of them were so poor that they couldn't get enough to eat and had diseases that could be cured as well as some that couldn't. Antonia traveled to many different countries to meet health workers, to educate people about health and nutrition, and to report back to the United Nations. She was the United Nations' representative to the World Health Organization and the 47th World Health Assembly.

In 1996 Antonia took a job as a director of community health policy in the Johns Hopkins School of Hygiene and Public Health. She is also a visiting professor in the School of Health Policy and Management. In her post Antonia continues her devotion to the improvement of health care and the education of health professionals.

CHRONOLOGY

1821   Elizabeth Blackwell is born near Bristol, England. Clara Barton is born in North Oxford, Massachusetts.

1841   Lucy Way Say, an entomologist, is the first woman elected to the male Academy of Natural Sciences, Philadelphia.

1848   Maria Mitchell, who discovered a new comet, is the first woman at the American Academy of Arts and Sciences in Boston.

1850   Lydia Folger Fowler receives her M.D. from Central Medical College; the second woman to become a doctor in the United States. Quaker physicians open the Female Medical College of Pennsylvania.

1859   Elizabeth Blackwell becomes the first female doctor in England when her name is entered on the Medical Register.

1862   Clara Barton receives a military pass and begins to distribute supplies to the front lines and serve as nurse.

1864   European nations sign the Treaty of Geneva. The International Red Cross is founded.

1865   Maria Mitchell, professor of astronomy at Vassar College, sets up an observatory and a program for women.

1865–69   Clara Barton forms an organization to find missing soldiers.

1868   Elizabeth Blackwell opens a medical school for women with strict entrance requirements and a four-year course of study.

1869   Howard University Medical School begins admitting women.

1870   The University of Michigan becomes the first state school to accept female medical students. Ellen Swallow (Richards) is the first woman admitted to the Massachusetts Institute of Technology; she opens a women's laboratory there in 1873.

1872   Dr. Mary Putman founds the Association for the Advancement of Medical Education of Women. The first U.S. nursing school is formed by Drs. Marie Zakrzewska and Susan Dimock; three more schools open in 1873.

1875   Emeline Cleveland removes an ovarian tumor and becomes the first U.S. woman to perform major surgery.

1878   Dr. Marie Zakrzewska is elected first president of the New England Hospital Medical Society after women are denied membership in Massachusetts medical society. Clara Barton delivers request to the president as a special representative of the International Red Cross.

1881   Clara Barton founds the American Red Cross Society.

1886   Rachel Lloyd becomes the first U.S. woman to receive a Ph.D. in chemistry, from the University of Zurich.

1898   Cornell University accepts women to study medicine; Elizabeth Blackwell's medical school closes (by 1903 only 3 of 17 women's medical schools remain open). Marie and Pierre Curie isolate and name radium and polonium.

1903   The Curies and Henri Becquerel share the Nobel Prize for physics.

1904   Clara Barton's activities as president of the Red Cross are investigated; she is cleared of all charges but resigns.

1907   Radium is added to the periodic table of the elements.

1908   Martha Minerva Franklin becomes president of the newly formed Colored Graduate Nurses, after black nurses were barred from membership in state and national organizations.

1911   Marie Curie wins the Nobel Prize for chemistry.

1916   Margaret Sanger, Ethel Byrne, and Fania Mindell open the first U.S. birth control clinic, in New York City.

1918   Frances Elliott (Davis) is the first black Red Cross Nurse. Rachel Carson's first short story is published.

1925   Marie Curie and other scientists issue a report about the health dangers of radioactivity. Margaret Mead begins fieldwork in Samoa. Rachel Carson enrolls in Pennsylvania College for Women.

1927   Margaret Mead becomes assistant curator of ethnology at American Museum of Natural History in New York.

1928   Mead publishes *Coming of Age in Samoa*.

1935   Irene Curie wins the Nobel Prize. Mead's *Sex and Temperament in Three Primitive Societies* is published.

1937   Rachel Carson's "Undersea" is published in *Atlantic Monthly*. The American Medical Association approves medical school courses in birth control.

1940   Elsie Clews Parsons elected first woman president of the American Anthropological Association.

1941   Margaret Mead and Gregory Bateson's *Balinese Character: A Photographic Analysis* is published. *Under the Sea-Wind* by Rachel Carson is published.

1944   Margaret Mead founds the Institute for Intercultural Studies at the American Museum of Natural History.

1945   Twelve women enter Harvard Medical School.

1949	The American Nurses' Association admits black nurses; the Colored Graduate Nurses group dissolves.
1951	Rachel Carson's *The Sea Around Us* is published.
1955	Rachel Carson's *The Edge of the Sea* is published.
1960	Dr. Nina Starr Braunwald becomes the first woman in the United States to perform open-heart surgery.
1961	Dr. Janet Graeme Travell is the first female White House physician, serving as John Kennedy's personal doctor.
1962	Rachel Carson's *Silent Spring* is published.
1965	Rachel Carson's *A Sense of Wonder* is published.
1969	The Women's Medical College of Pennsylvania admits men and becomes the Medical College of Philadelphia.
1971	The National Black Nurses' Association forms.
1980	Rachel Carson is posthumously awarded the Presidential Medal of Freedom.
1990–93	Antonia Novello becomes first woman and the first Latin American U.S. surgeon general.
1993–96	Antonia Novello becomes special representative for health and nutrition with UNICEF.

FURTHER READING

Anticaglia, Elizabeth. *Twelve American Women*. Chicago: Nelson Hall, 1975.

Barton, Clara. *The Story of My Childhood*. New York: Arno, 1980, reprint of 1907 edition.

Blackwell, Elizabeth. *Pioneer Work in Opening the Medical Profession to Women: Autobiographical Sketches*. New York: Schocken, 1977.

Brown, Ray, ed. *Contemporary Heroes and Heroines*. Detroit: Gale Research, 1990.

Burton, David. *Clara Barton: In the Service of Humanity*. Westport, Conn.: Greenwood, 1995.

Clapp, Patricia. *Dr. Elizabeth: The Story of the First Woman Doctor*. New York: Lothrop, Lee, and Shepard, 1974.

Hawxhurst, Joan C. *Antonia Novello: U.S. Surgeon General*. Brookfield, Conn.: Millbrook, 1993.

Lear, Linda. *Rachel Carson: Witness for Nature*. New York: Holt, 1997.

Ludel, Jacqueline. *Margaret Mead*. New York and London: Franklin Watts, 1983.

Lunt, Elizabeth. "Elizabeth Blackwell (1821–1910): Physician." In *Notable Women in the Life Sciences: A Biographical Dictionary*, ed. Benjamin Shearer and Barbara Shearer. Westport, Conn.: Greenwood, 1996.

Mead, Margaret. "Field Work in the Pacific Islands, 1925–1967." In *Women in the Field: Anthropological Experiences*, ed. Peggy Golde. Chicago: Aldine, 1970.

Mead, Margaret. *Blackberry Winter: My Earlier Years*. New York: Morrow, 1972.

Oates, Stephen B. *A Woman of Valor: Clara Barton and the Civil War*. New York: Free Press, 1994.

Quinn, Susan. *Marie Curie: A Life*. New York and London: Simon and Schuster, 1995.

Reynolds, Moira Davison. *Immigrant American Women Role Models*. Jefferson, N.C.: McFarland, 1997.

Rodda, Arlene. "Rachel Carson (1907–1964): Biologist, Environmentalist." In *Notable Women in the Life Sciences: A Biographical Dictionary*, ed. Benjamin Shearer and Barbara Shearer. Westport, Conn.: Greenwood, 1996.

INDEX

ABOUT THE AUTHOR

Gina De Angelis holds a bachelor of arts degree in theater and a master of arts in history. She is the author of several plays and screenplays as well as five titles for Chelsea House. Currently an archaeological intern, she lives with her daughter—and three gerbils—in Williamsburg, Virginia.